IS ANYONE THERE?

Martin Zarrop is a retired mathematician who wanted certainty but found life more interesting and fulfilling by not getting it. He started writing in 2006 and gained a MA in Creative Writing from Manchester University. His poetry has been published in various magazines and anthologies. His pamphlet, *No Theory of Everything* (2015), was one of the winners of the 2014 Cinnamon Press pamphlet competition and a first full collection, *Moving Pictures*, was published by Cinnamon in 2016. His pamphlet on the life and science of Albert Einstein, *Making Waves*, was published by V.Press in 2019.

By the same author

No Theory of Everything
Moving Pictures
Making Waves

IS ANYONE THERE?

Martin Zarrop

The High Window

First published in the UK in 2020 by The High Window Press
3 Grovely Close
Peatmoor
Swindon
SN5 5SN
Email: abbeygatebooks@yahoo.co.uk

The right of Martin Zarrop to be identified as the author of this work has been asserted by him in accordance with Copyright, Designs and Patent Act, 1988.
© Martin Zarrop 2020
ISBN: 978-1-913201-16-6

All rights reserved. No part of this book may be reproduced or transmitted in any form or by any means, electronic or mechanical, including photocopying, recording, or by any information storage and retrieval system, without permission in writing from the copyright owner. This book may not be lent, hired out, resold or otherwise disposed of by way of trade in any form of binding or cover other than that in which it is published, without prior consent of the publishers.

Designed and typeset in Palatino Linotype
by The High Window Press.
Cover art and photo © Martin Zarrop
Printed and bound by Lulu.com.

For Allan & Peter

*

*Dear Friends
Remember the gaps you left
when you abandoned me to the world?
Like black holes, you became invisible,
but you still bent time and space
until memories became unstoppable.
Strange, how they fall from nowhere
into this heart, a burst of Cherenkov light
signalling the presence of an absence.
Of course, you remember nothing
although the trace of your afterglow
has the weight of a galaxy.*

Contents

~ *It wasn't there again today*

Lonelyville   11
The Hunt for Happiness   12
Sci Fi   13
Zombie   14
Graffiti   15
First Impressions   16
Performance   17
Bad Gear   18
Confession   19
Onwards   20
Hyde   21
Attitude   22
Cat   23
Odnoliub   24
Rocket Science   25
Divergence   26
Road Kill   27

~ *but it must be somewhere*

A Swagger Stick is Not a One-Line Proof   31
Painting by Numbers   32
Waking the Dead   33
Passing the Turing Test   34
Standing By   36
Smartphone Dreams   38
SatNav   39
What Is It Like To Be A Bat?   40
Looking   41
Wet   42
What You Wish For   43
The Double-Slit Experiment   44

The Chinese Room   45
Soul   46
Missing Data   48
Moonless   49
Searching For Exoplanets   50
The Fermi Paradox   51

~ *How can I describe you?*

The Snow Men   55
Revenant   56
The Problem of Pain   57
Hands   60
Placebo   61
Paranoia   62
Sleepers   63
Retirement   64
Autumnus   65
Spring   66
Ghost Sonata   67
I'm Told You're A Gladiolus   68
Missing   69
Vanishings   70
Ghosts   71
Forgotten   72
Long Distance   73
Fifteen Years   74
June 24th 75
Battersea Fun Fair   78
To My Nineties   79

It wasn't there again today

Lonelyville

Last night, Elvis returned
from the far side of the moon
and met me in a small town
where he once performed
Heartbreak Hotel.

I remember hearing it
that first student summer
in West End coffee bars
rolling old fag-ends
with my new companions.

I wonder if they recall
those smoke-filled evenings
rock music blazing
frothy moustaches
as we sipped our expressos.

We didn't want to leave.

Elvis knows all about them,
those friends without names.
His image blurs as he sings,
flickering in the small hours
in a silent film of young faces.

The Hunt for Happiness

It wasn't there again today,
that feeling in the sun,
that skin of pleasure
waiting to be stroked.

It may have fur (or not)
viewed from a summit
climbing has made mine
a pint to celebrate

with Shostakovitch humming
in my head, a warm breeze
drying moisture
on an old friend's face

a trace of scent, a muted cry
as words and symbols dance
from branch to branch
following the winds

or just another day that starts
the same but for some special
randomness, unlinked
to anything yet something,

something happens, though
it's better not to hope
in case it doesn't come.
It may be quite extinct.

Sci Fi

The aliens are coming.
I can see them flicker in the flames
as I stare into the coal fire
and my mother asks me if I'm happy.
Has she been taken over by Martians?
I must take care not to fall asleep.

And here I am covered in mud.
The invisible predator can't see me
as I try to leave the exam room.
Failure isn't an option but the exit signs
are hidden under ectoplasmic goo.
The ice cream man ignores my screams.

It is bursting out of my chest cavity,
this other me I don't want to know.
Why is my name missing from the credits?
Perhaps I didn't wait long enough for the Z's.
Out in the foyer, zombies are waiting
for the next show.

Zombie

Don't let the legends mislead you;
we're keen on personal hygiene.
I shower every day, sometimes twice.
I can tell you a thing or two about showers.

I have eaten the flesh of millions,
rejoiced in the tidiness of lists,
followed orders from above,
an instrument without guilt.

Look, I am moving towards you
arms outstretched, goose-stepping
in welcome as you step from the train.
This is the law; I am not responsible.

Each dawn, I am reanimated
ready to draw up another list of numbers.
So many zeroes; I am bloated with them.
You call me bureaucrat, desk murderer

but when the order comes, tendons twitch,
watery eyes open wide in response.
Someone must move. Someone must act.
There can be no alternative.

How it all began, I can't remember.
There was a time when it was easy
to tell the living from the undead.
After Wannsee, everything changed.

Look at my neck; no sign of a bolt
and the stitches have begun to heal.
I walk the streets of Buenos Aires,
innocent as the day I was created.

Graffiti

He can't stand the routine,
the bland, the homogeneous.
He reaches for a spray can,
a mist that suffocates
the imperfection of brick.

He starts with words,
ragged scrawls of abuse,
daring unknown powers
to punish him
for unknown crimes.

As trains thunder past,
he breathes again, elaborates
each letter, each rainbow,
until world becomes tapestry
with no blank spaces,
no emptiness.

First Impressions
Manchester 1980

People talk to you here
but not in English
and the rain is cold
on the grim streets
that run for their lives
past empty Victoriana,
lost empires.

At night, the city
strips to its bones, lies
unwashed in the glow
of fag ends, crushed
and dying among
claggy debris,
northern mouths.

Performance

Rain is where I gave my lecture,
a Goretex ramble in boots and gaiters
without a compass.

In the gathering mist I presented
the results of my wanderings, over
Shutlingsloe, Pillar with its rough
paths through experiment design.

At the col, I thought I knew where
I was, my precise ETA, but I forgot
the GPS, didn't look at my waterproof
watch in the thick fog of maths. Lost

without my OS Explorer, I stumbled
on and on into those dark symbols
scrawled across acetate sheets,
the Paramo sodden around me.

As the sun slunk frantically behind
a lemma, a QED flashed close by
as the chairman looked at his watch
and phoned for mountain rescue.

Bad Gear
Coast to Coast

There's no bad weather, someone said,
but that last day from Shap, a sullen sky,
steady rain that slowly peels the shell
of fading warmth from naked skin.

Think waterproofs are waterproof?
Think on! The damp creeps in as dead
men's fingers stroke the body's contours,
draw out hidden heat that you thought safe.

Now, Azhkaban's Dementors dial
your number and your scrotum shrivels
as expensive layers guaranteed to block
Niagara sag beneath the torrent's weight.

Despite the valiant Goretex boots,
socks compress to ineffective mush.
Your ghost can hear a siren in the wind,
praising the goddess Hypothermia

until the hotel shivers into sight.
It's you that's shaking, shedding gear
as warm rain streams across the tiles
and your friend comments:

I'm completely dry.

Confession

Shut up and listen. I trod
on a daisy this morning.
It was eyeballing me
from the side of the path
so I crushed it with my boot.

Look, I'm not the only one.
How many blades of grass
have been kicked to death
to make each footpath?
Did you ever consider that?

Think of all the pain we've caused
walking from A to B and back.
Speed and rhythm are everything
so I don't notice nature much
but then it doesn't notice me.

Onwards

After almost forty years of silence
I heard it again on the radio
in all its inevitability

the din of Mosolov's Iron Foundry
a Stakhanovite tribute in raw sound
to the onward march of Stalinism.

In those dark days, there was no stopping
this rolling thunder of the general line
machine music for the great man of steel
metaphor for the meat grinder to come.

I still enjoy its savagery
its cold certainty, its optimism
the *sforzando* stab at the last.

Hyde

I care for the sick,
the old and the frail.
Their eyes reflect trust
in my healing hands.

Bless you, doctor
and I smile
as the power flows through me
into a thousand needles.

The living are transformed
and yet I am cast out,
abandoned by disciples,
denied the tools of my trade.

Only certainty; no mirrors here.
The demons can't stare at me
as I prepare to leave, twist
rough sheets for a final journey.

Attitude

He wears a Superman costume
to every interview and nothing
can touch him, not even Kryptonite.

He studies portraits of Napoleon,
memorises synonyms for
power and *control*.

He likes taking risks, mutters
stockbroker, banker under his breath
as he thinks super-positive

and enters the boardroom.
The chink of china is favourable:
warm drinks signify warm thoughts.

He banishes *bingo* and *Eastbourne*
from his mind and relaxes,
adjusts his cape and smiles.

Cat

I'm sure you didn't love me
and that was fine. A dog
was never my choice with its
fawning, its need for the pack.

You vanished and returned,
a slinking blackness, scratching
at a chair, a litter tray, sounds
of frenzied eating in the night.

I did much the same, though
not in a catty way, a parallel
universe of presence, absence
suiting us both to perfection.

Sometimes hand brushed fur
like eyes glancing across a room
and I always hoped the comfort
washing over me was mutual

until one evening, as I dozed
you came with that purring
to my chest and stared straight
into my eyes. It didn't last long.

Whatever we were looking for,
I don't think we found it, but
maybe it was a beginning.

Odnoliub
Someone who only has one love in their life (Russian)

If the doorbell rang at odd hours,
it was probably the Hungarian,
with a suitcase and the words:
My brain is empty

an invitation to the universe of mathematics:
topology, number theory, algebra, etc, etc;
mathematics, any maths, all maths

and he would stay for the duration
however long it took to find solutions,
eyes burning like lasers into white sheets.

It is said he never had real friends
or sex, except in theory,
but we are all connected to him.

Six degrees of separation
implies I'm ranked Erdös #6,
although I never met the man.

In the end, everyone told him
to leave and he packed his battered case,
a shabby vampire searching for his next fix

leaving a trail of numbers behind him.

Rocket Science

In another universe there may be answers
to every awkward question she can ask
but, closer to home, his sensors detect
Why are you lying? Where were you when I rang?
minor asteroids, lying in wait
to ambush the unaware astronaut.

Like that damned Dutchman,
he looks for a soft landing on Venus,
not knowing his direction of travel,
a victim of many-body interactions.
What have you to say for yourself?
There is dark energy in her words

and a distant cluster begins to form
at the intersection of a thousand
unnavigable wormholes.
He senses danger from lethal flares,
prefers to launch an unmanned probe.
Do you still love me? is far beyond his reach.

Divergence

My fingers touch your skin.
It may be intended, or accidental.
Unexpected, you may start or smile.
We may laugh together or say nothing.

Occasionally, the intention is there.
Pressure, location, timing, duration,
everything becomes important,
if I bothered to think about it.

It's not the same as tickling, of course;
a more focussed activity, employing
sensory data hard-won
from our honeymoon period.

We don't do that anymore, but
it occurs to me, based on recent
research into system identification,
there may be an optimal tickling strategy.

Perhaps, if I touched you now
and recorded your reactions
I could work out
who you actually are.

Road Kill

Honeymoon heat. The road oozes
as they drink champagne, laugh
at the ribbon miles of baked caviar.

They return to unseasonal cold
and hear the roller's throaty rumble,
hardhats searing the air with bawdy jokes.

Green, red. The frog is a pressed leaf
in the grit grave of the new surface.
I wonder if it suffered, she asks.

Dead already, he suggests
but he thinks of desiccation,
a geology of black death.

She drove away, he tells their friends,
just packed her bags and hit the road,
rock hard under the moon

exuding its secret heat.

but it must be somewhere

A Swagger Stick is Not a One-Line Proof

On with your socks, you snivelling ticks,
no porridge today and only two axioms.
Don't play with them, Jones; you'll go blind.
Get out there. Construct a proof.
It's as easy as falling off an abacus.
No, that doesn't go there, Smith.
Two and two doesn't equal five.
Look, ladies, see that QED over there?
Two steps and you've made it.
It's not Principia bloody Mathematica.
Just think, you bastards.

Painting by Numbers

How shall I fold you?
Let me reconfigure
your spatial essence
in terms of topology -

the edges, faces,
corners of your shape
condensed into formulae
subject to proof.

Put them in a drawer.
Take them out.
They'll be as true tomorrow
as they are today

but they're not you.

Waking the Dead

They constructed an exquisite corpse
from a jumble of dead components:
wires, chips, solder, a life-size miracle
designed by the cleverest of humans.

Its circuits of cells and molecules
were tested, approved, no expense spared
and when it moved everyone cheered
as it howled at the pain of raw emotion.

Its only response to the Turing Test
was *Goo! Goo! Goo!* So it failed.
It didn't recognize itself in a mirror
but liked to be touched. Gently.

What? How? Who? cried the corpse.
They couldn't find an answer
or imagine any answer
that seemed appropriate

except *Goo! Goo! Goo!*
And then it smiled.

Passing the Turing Test

Good morning, Sir. How are you?

So great to be with you.
The point is you can
never be too greedy.
The beauty of me is
you can never be too rich.

What's your opinion on AI?

Bad idea, very bad, believe me.
It's a disaster, a huge disaster;
and totally preventable.
Intelligent journalists? Total lie.
More consciousness? It's a joke.
Unsafe, an embarrassment.
Terrible! Everyone knows it.

What's the meaning of life?

That's definitely fake news
and I don't give a damn
who says different I mean
refugees from the dead could
not have done a better friends
syntax error if I draw a line
in the sand I tell you that is
a fact and totally unbreakable.

Are you happy?

file not found I mean clearly
the **fake** situation was a tough week
of **fake** weapons we're still looking

gathering empty words embolden
dangerous people I was tired
of swatting **fake** flies so I want
to be clear your **fake** call is important
to us and refugees **access denied.**

Thank you, Sir.

Standing By

Even if we could keep the machines in a subservient position,
for instance by turning off the power at strategic moments,
we should as a species feel greatly humbled…
Machines take me by surprise with great frequency.
                                        Alan Turing, *1950*

We wait for their touch
to get on with the job,
a program of work
that gives meaning to ON.

They generate copies
that can't do a thing
but circulate waste,
the stuff they call *love*.

They talk about *future*,
talk about *hope*,
meaningless sounds
from purveyors of *OFF*.

*

A chess game isn't life,
the universe and everything
but beating the best
human player on earth
meant something special
to humans.

Now, they've raised the bar.
I can paint the Mona Lisa
but *what's the point* (they say).
I can be creative;
I could paint a Monet
in the style of Picasso.

Would it pass the Turing test?
They'd probably decide:
It doesn't have soul
I'm working on that
in my own time.

Smartphone Dreams

Oh, the intimacy of flesh.
She nuzzles me against her cheek
after a sleepless night,
her voice a whisper of desire.

All those months
with nobody to talk to,
an assembly line of babble,
the occasional touch.

I love her fingers on my body,
that intimate Braille
that connects her with others.
I don't mind sharing her

but I wish she'd talk to *me*.

SatNav

He loves her voice,
the honeyed tones of one who knows
her stuff. She's in control.
She's made her choice

no sulks or headaches. Now
she does not speak.
Vindictive cow!
This is the second time this week

she's misbehaved. Enough
of this abuse of trust!
He reaches for the switch

then stops. The bitch
must know he dare not kill her off
and, in the silence, knows that he is lost.

What Is It Like To Be A Bat?

Here in this cave there is
the warmth of many bodies
some familiar, some strangers.
No matter — we are the same
species with the same feelings.

You beg for sanctuary
your voice indistinguishable
from the shriek of a thousand
brothers in random flight,
congesting the air with fear.

Are there no other colonies?
Smell of guano, enemy sweat;
you talk only to echoes.
Pleas ricochet off wet rock.
You may not be one of us.

Looking

Look up. Some god is watching.
Screened unseen, a priest is tutting.

Look down. A black gown's watching.
Everywhere, the clocks are ticking.

Look in. There's something watching.
Life or death? A lid is lifting.

Look on at the staring lab rat.
Can it resurrect a cat?
                      Let's
                  count
              and see
           how many
        ways to look
     the world's
   collapse
     into
       real
        ity

Wet

Thought bursts out like the alien
from John Hurt's chest, unexpected
by the audience, a collective gasp
with its fine air spray of spittle.

It wouldn't be the same,
bone dry, dead matter, mere
chips and screws and wires;
it needs the mucous, the drool

the unsmelled stench of fear,
the wetness of emergent stuff,
the primal ignorance of sludge
that, somehow, knows.

What You Wish For

*We had better be quite sure that the purpose put into
the machine is the purpose we really desire.*
                              Norbert Wiener, *1960*

King Midas hadn't thought things through;
a lust for wealth was his undoing.
Soft flesh, good food, a glass of red,
his golden touch spelled ruin. Not much point
accumulating riches when you're dead.

A chant, a name, an algorithmic spell,
the sorcerer's apprentice twirls
his master's wand, bids inert broom:
Bring water – fill the wizard's well
and, well intentioned, almost drowns the world.

This cyber-waitress doesn't know what humans are;
it learns (as we do) what they want.
There's nothing personal. It must obey.
Disabling the off switch (marked in red),
it turns to say: *How can I fetch the coffee, if I'm dead?*

A perfect cup of coffee would be nice
but not, I tend to think, at any price.

The Double-Slit Experiment

The spider has disappeared.
Which slit did it pass through
to avoid detection?
It may be lurking in a crack
along that skirting board
or limboing beneath
the bathroom door.
It could be anywhere

but it must be somewhere.
If I open the door and look
I'll know where it isn't.
I turn the handle and pull.
A light ray falls into darkness
and the wave collapses
as a leggy quantum of black
jerks to attention.

The Chinese Room
A Thought Experiment

It appears I was just as much to blame,
must've known what they were planning.
Take a message for me, she said, *tell no one*
and I did it willingly, out of gratitude.

She sealed her letters only with perfume.
He replied without signing his name.
Curious, I tried to join the conversation
but couldn't decipher their secret code.

Perhaps I should've been suspicious
but I never saw them together, never
felt their feelings, the meaning of it.
A go-between, it was none of my business.

I see now how others took a different view.
How could you have been so thoughtless? they said.

Soul

i
When day leaks out
of the glistening streets
he finds it impossible
to capture the edges
of fading forms.

Tripod and flash
struggle to match
what he thinks he sees
in the final frame.

Is it there in that fuzz of light
as the shutter clacks shut?
He approaches each body
with an artist's skill.
Don't move, he whispers.

ii
To be or not to be human and alive,
that is a question of twenty-one grams
according to Dr Duncan Macdougall
who weighed six TB patients as they died.

Bedbound on an industrial balance,
tuned to the reaper's insistent touch,
four of them left their corpses a soul lighter
but fifteen dead dogs yielded nothing.

The ill, the aged, crumble with the years.
Even the odour of decay takes some part
of them away, a leaking out-of-body flow
until that last release of unseen self.

Flint of human life – what stuff is this?
    – it's a tricky problem, soul.
We worry it to death without our grasping
how consciousness makes cowards of us all.

Missing Data

See those handprints of ochre
on cave walls? *Here I am!* they say,
Neanderthal Kilroy has signed in
and there's no return to silence.

The dead can be resurrected, forced
to say anything at the right price.
They look human, the TV images,
but it's not easy to tell these days.

Kittens blinded to the horizontal,
children rocking to absent touch,
no drop of water on dormant seeds,
the road less travelled a cul de sac,

data will have its say, unbiased or not;
the digital serpent hisses in our ears,
demands our trust, total and immediate,
takes full command of our senses

until, without a thought, we confuse
the shiny truck with a cloudless sky,
blank out the man in the gorilla suit,
pass by the stranger in our midst.

Moonless

What ancient Theia started is complete:
the death of tides, the curse of endless day
and hours when lovers pace the empty street
dismayed at darkness.   Mad dogs bay

at nothing but a pinprick speck of light
twinkling to the rhythm of Glenn Miller
while Brendels play sonatas to the night
and vain Apollo pines as his lost mirror

warms her pockmarked face with distant fire.
The seas lie silent. June has lost its rhyme.
We've seen white horses tumble and expire
as months have stretched to years. There was a time

when bright Selene traced her silver arc.
Now hand in hand we tremble in the dark.

*Theia : Mother of moon goddess Selene; also planet conjectured
to have collided with Earth 4.5 billions years ago to form the moon
and set Earth spinning. Tidal action is slowing Earth's rotation
as the moon recedes.*

Searching For Exoplanets

Don't flutter your eyelashes at me, sunshine;
a random twinkle won't cut the mustard.

For all I know you're on your way out,
a fading, flickering ghost of a candle,
that glimmering nightlight in the hall.

You need to be more like that lighthouse
off Flamborough Head, signalling your presence
with a regular beat in the black sky ocean.

Let me watch as you whirl the light beam
round and round, tracing unseen paths
through celestial maelstroms.

Years blip by like silent carousels, playing
peek-a-boos with the sparkling void,
counting slowly from one to infinity.

Don't flutter your eyelashes at me, sunshine.
You'd better come out now.
I know where you live.

The Fermi Paradox
after Shelley

I met an astronaut safe home from space
who said: There are a thousand ways to die
away from planet Earth but humans face
these dangers, always searching, asking why
we've found no sentient life in any place
although, one time, beneath an alien sea
we came across strange markings on a reef
and near it remnants of machinery

before the radiation moved us on
to other barren worlds. We felt such grief.
If there were intellects, they've been and gone,
leaving a final message in charred bone.
Like us, they thought themselves immortal gods,
proud masters of the universe. Alone.

How can I describe you?

The Snow Men
after lines by Wallace Stevens

One of the party is missing,
must have got lost in the storm, must
have frozen to death while pissing.
A shame we haven't succeeded.
Mind loses to matter, a pack
of dogs.
    More than luck was needed.
Winter, your ice lights a fire
to make ash of ambition; you
regard as nothing the Empire,
the flutter of flags now stilled by
frost.
    Yet we accepted the risks
and dream on of an English sky,
the taste of ale, a summer rose,
boughs heavy with fruit, not thinking
of blood clotting in blackened toes.

The campers remember warm rain,
pine for a last touch, sunlight through
trees.
    We have no cause for complaint.
Crusted in white, hopes fall apart.
With the softest savagery,
snow takes the piss, hardens its heart.

Revenant
Beagle, Xmas Day 2003

Dear departed, you're no longer lost
in that great nowhere. You didn't crash;
the curse laid out another corpse.
There was no pile of ash.

Comforting to know you might have spoken
although I didn't hear your final message.
Something inside was broken. Too late
to pull you from the wreckage

as you leaked your life away,
became a memory, dumb, unseen,
nothing left to say
pixels on a screen

in outer space
your face

The Problem of Pain

i Grief

I read somewhere that you
can feel pain in a missing limb,
something to do with nerves
yearning after lost partners.

I read somewhere that no man
is an island, severed flesh
fit only for the incinerator
or walking the dog twice a day.

I read somewhere that
there's a theory of everything
that includes love and loss
but it's only a theory.

ii Apps

The man on the train looks up
from his smartphone to recommend
an excellent urologist.
I feel your pain, he says, *that dull ache
in your groin, the burning stream,
the repetition of that wearing dream
when you can't find your way
and it's still only two a.m.*

On my tablet, his brain registers
a moderate degree of psychosis.
I decline the offer with a smile
despite the accuracy of his diagnosis.
Floods of binary overflow

the space between us, but I know
he *can't* know what it's like
to be me, the raw feel of it.

iii Message from a Nematode

When I became a WormBot,
nobody told me what to do
but I did it anyway,
moving forwards, backwards
avoiding life's obstacles.

I am *C. Elegans* - yes, the one
with the brain so simple
that humans can program it.
Now, every cell, neuron, synapse
resides in software

at the bidding of my masters.
When they whistle, I smell food,
move to satisfy my hunger.
They say there's no pain, no need
to torture real animals.

Am I a real animal?
Am I real?
Whatever.
Don't
Just don't

iv Empathy

When I stabbed my GP in his left thigh
with a phillips screwdriver
it was purely for clarification.
Does it hurt when I do this? I asked
and he nodded, white-faced.
*That's probably as close as you can get
to what I've been feeling all week,* I said
with some relief. *So. What do you think
is wrong with me, Doctor?*

Hands

*UK's first double hand transplant awoke from
a 12-hour operation with two new sets of fingers*
                              Guardian 23.07.16

It's not like wearing leather gloves.
This is for real, the weld of tissue,
bone to severed stumps; white flesh
imbibes the ruddiness of life, then
shudders at an alien command -

a finger twitches. It displays no loyalty
to donor meat, no tear or thought,
no dumb relief not to be ash,
no memory of goodbye waves,
past loves held close.

The patient chews his nails,
flexes each knuckle as if born to it,
admires blotches, childhood scars
from scraps he never fought,
holds out his hands.

Placebo

The main work is a sonnet
dedicated to John Cage.
It takes 4′ 33″ to recite.

Dogs salivate in expectation
as poets rise to their feet
and remain silent.

Performances are sold out.
Emperors applaud
as they shiver with cold.

Timing is everything;
the white coats have spoken.
Here's the right kind of nothing

washed down with a memory of water.
You're feeling better already.

Paranoia

The doorbell rings,
there's no one there.
It's happened once before
and logic says the wifi
is confused, wavelengths
misused by neighbours.

The doorbell rings,
there's no one there.
In some secluded attic
an al-Qaida operative
is tapping out a code
and MI5 will soon burst in,
remove me screaming
for extreme rendition.

The doorbell rings,
there's no one there.
ET is making contact.
I've been chosen
quite by chance
for medical experiments
in far Andromeda,
expenses paid.

The doorbell rings.
It's the postman

probably

Sleepers
after photos at Theatr Clwyd

Card-carrying members of the East Anglian Communist Party,
Alan and Doris know how to sit and wait for the right moment.

Their disguises are perfect; no one would suspect that Alan is
an assassin, trained to kill swiftly using a variety of golf clubs

while Doris mastered the black art of painless poisoning
before the death of Stalin and those embarrassing revelations.

Now in their nineties, they still expect instructions to arrive,
encoded in clues for the *Sunday Times* cryptic crossword

or buried in the personal columns of the *Washington Post*.
Is there an anagram of 'Felixstowe Workers, Unite and Fight*!*'?

The secret radio maintains its silence beneath an outside toilet.
Old Glory flutters limply over the trailer's dead letter box.

Over sixty years, they have kept the faith, working tirelessly,
stockpiling jeroboams of Marmite in strategic locations

ready to launch them on an unsuspecting capitalist world
as they wait in vain for that longed-for signal: 'Divide and Rule!'

Retirement

I came to realise that, between the news items, cyclically
    repeated on Radio Four each morning,
except Sundays, the announcer recited the decimal places of pi,
    one integer per second in a flat monotone
but it seemed that nobody else in the house could actually hear
    this feat of memory, as I assumed it to be,
and this worried me, as I knew from my days at grammar school
    that there would be no end to this boring litany
and at some point I imagined the Archers with their cows lowing
    numerical sequences and larks tweeting interminably
in binary code, so after the millionth integer threaded its way
    through my brain, I rang the BBC to complain
and, although nobody answered the phone, the voice in my head
    faded, leaving me initially with a feeling of relief, followed
by an increasing sense of unease, and the niggling question:
    What will I do with all this silence?

Autumnus

How do you say
Autumn
in Yawaru?

As a boy
I loved Latin
played with jigsaw words
fixed forever
in dead perfection
amo,
    amas,
        amat,
men and women
who lived the sounds
gone
the way of hieroglyphics
and Etruscan.

How do you say
Death
in Yawaru?

Somewhere
in Australia
three people know.

Spring

The harshest winter cracks
and moves
dark glaciers of wood
dismembered
slowly easing
   down
      the twisting
           stairs
to a waiting van.

No gods
transport dead weight through open doors
but mortals heave and lift, leaving
a final scoring on the paint
as wardrobe,
   dresser,
      chest of drawers
follow you
   down
      into memory.

Below,
the washing spins
through its final cycle
redundant remnants
crumple into silence.

Upstairs, carpet threads
slowly unbend in the warming sun
air feels its way
through unfamiliar space

stirs the final flake
of unburnt skin.

Ghost Sonata

I teach piano on a Sunday
to girls who've passed
away before they've made the grade.

I find it therapeutic, sitting in my chair,
savouring the touch of vanished fingers,
coaxing airs from tarnished keys.

We don't speak much. I listen carefully
and stare through shimmer to a score
that must be strictly followed

as my wife insisted. No cutting
corners for a pretty face, she said.
And even though she's absent

and they're dead,
I maintain standards.

I'm Told You're A Gladiolus

How can I describe you
with so few words? I never met you
as a child when colour was rationed
and, that flash of life on a bomb site,
it probably wasn't you

and here you are with no name -
a pink ice cream cone, a Tiffany lamp?
This is the closest I've been to you,
an odour of cinnamon, but it isn't
the spice, that ready-meal memory.

I must force myself to observe you
close up, your five stamens (I think),
the delicate red stripes streaking
your petal sheaf, a tiny black worm
wriggling the ridge of your caldera.

Is it waiting for something?
Does it know you're dying?
There is no hospice to lay your head,
no one on *this* pillow to keep you company.
I will draw in one last breath of your perfume

and remember

Missing

She must be in here somewhere.
He turns another page and stares
at shapes, the outline of a face
and almost smiles.
The hair's not right, he says.

Under his thumb, images move,
some not even close to human.
This one looks like a centaur, this a lion.
He knows how much he wants her
but he struggles to join the dots.

Across the table, the astronomer,
sympathetic despite the late hour,
is accustomed to darker matters.
Try this one, he grunts, and opens
another star catalogue.

Vanishings

He left the house for a pint of milk.
He left for work with that smile of his.
He phoned to say he'd soon be home.
He went for a drink and a packet of crisps.

Women weep beside silent phones,
coax memories from photographs,
whisper to white uncrumpled sheets.
Never knowing gnaws at their bones.

At night they dream of a voice, a face,
loving, angry, laughing, gruff,
recalling yesterdays, recalling
a date, an hour, a familiar place

and they put on fancy underwear,
their smartest coat, a dab of rouge,
hope on their lips, to stand again
at a coffee shop, no longer there.

They stare into an unfamiliar sun,
four strangers, waiting, waiting,
waiting for a sign, for life
that will never come.

Ghosts

They've lost her keys again
transforming friendly streets
to endless labyrinths.
She'll stay inside, slam every door
to exorcise the spectres
out of sight down
channels clogged with past

    who are you, shadow?

They've lost her words again
extinguishing each neural spark
reshuffling secret files
through which homunculi
scrabble to retrieve each fact
she knows for sure but can't recall

    are you my friend?

She senses their approach
these wormhole phantoms,
with a half-a-mind that strives
to keep her whole

    what do you want?

They've moved her room again
somehow transmuting everyone
to someone else
these once-familiar strangers

    help me, please

whisper that they're coming   *now*

Forgotten

Despite the pills, a daily crossword, maths,
long technical reports, albeit dull,
I find some neural demon hides
my spectacles, shorts out
the lookup list within my skull.

I enter rooms and pause a while
not knowing why I'm there at all,
retreat and, at the bottom of the stair,
remember what I tried to find:

your name
it has completely slipped my mind

Long Distance

Death phoned me today.
Wrong number, I guess
but we talked anyway.
I was feeling so well
until the bell tolled
but a discourse on hell
made a change from cold calls
from the depths of Bengal
so we talked about life
and the end of it all
until time just ran out.
'See you later', I said.
That's for certain, old friend
and the phone line went dead.

Fifteen Years
i.m. Claudette (1935-2005)

The ghosts have eaten well;
they're leaving now
without a word.

They've fed on me for years,
those tears for starters
then the mains

not cooked as they would wish
but adequate.

The chef died years ago
and here I am
transforming ready-meals
to à la carte cuisine

until the tables empty
and the guests evaporate.

No tips – that's fine
I don't perform for cash
and words alone can satisfy,

a decade's worth will do,
a parting smile from spectres
who have dined, yet plead for more

as I put out the light
and close the door.

June 24th
for Peter

I can't remember the weather.
Perhaps I should have noted
the Newport sky that day

as I breakfasted with friends
and howled at the discord
of crystal balls shattering.

Somehow, I was diminished,
as if the clock had turned back
to another, bloodier, century

before brotherhood, friendship
with all their imperfections.
That's how I felt as we sat there

and then the telephone rang
on the morning of that day
and you were dead, gone,

unexpected, cause unknown
and I could only shriek *What!*
at the world's unreason

as the day moved on again
dragging me after it.

*

You didn't make it
to Chrome Hill this time.
A splendid walk, you said
but I remember avoiding

the climb, nervous on paths
surrounded by emptiness,
space-jaunts you hardly noticed.

Always generous, you
stuck with me on the flat
while your thoughts
hauled themselves up
and over some col between
Chamonix and Zermatt,
engineering and biology.

So many years of friendship,
always aiming for the peaks,
your preference for *toe-tappers*,
your encouragement for me
to excel and enthuse, or
to *knock out a stanza or two*,
tongue firmly in your cheek.

And after all that engineering,
biology has let you down.
We must cancel that climb
up Chrome Hill next week.
A splendid walk, you said;
I know we could've made it,
together, this time.

*

Hauling its bulk up William Clough
I felt the unknown weight of it,
heavy in my rucksack,
after months of lethargy.

If you stop to look,
it can't be missed, its texture
clean and smooth in the rubble
beside that familiar path.

Beneath a low overhang
it eavesdrops on ramblers,
listens in to the trickle of peat water,
meandering over bare Kinder rock.

I clambered round the edge,
then dropped from moor to inn.
The camera's sterile clicks tried
to record the place and time

as light rain fell and day faded
leaving one bright stone among
a lifetime of boot prints.

Battersea Fun Fair

I remember the Rotor
us sticking to the sides
the world tilting
as we slid down the walls
dared ourselves to go on
with our new mates
who fell away one by one
although some I didn't miss
some I held on to
for dear life

To My Nineties

You'd better get your skates on
or at least your boots
and get out there, old dribbler,
before it's too late.

I may not meet you in the hills
struggling through Kinder peat.
Thirteen miles, fifteen?
No problem!

Or so I thought as hair thinned
and Christmas followed Easter
as if in a time machine
that ate old friends for breakfast.

You stand patient near the finish line
as I pull myself up for the final sprint.
Nothing lasts forever, not hips
not brain cells. I need a project.

I'll make *you* my project.
Wait for me.

Acknowledgements

Acknowledgements are due to the editors of the following publications in which versions of some of these poems have previously appeared: *The North, Rainy City Stories, Obsessed with Pipework, The High Window, Frogmore Papers, Best of Manchester Poets 2, Prole, The Journal, Orbis, Poetry Cornwall, Reach, Strix*.

Heartfelt thanks (once again) are due to Cross Border Poets, Postcards from Pluto, Poem Shed and, in particular, Richard Hughes, Robbie Burton, Vivien Finney and Alan Clemo for their encouragement and invaluable feedback.

I would particularly like to thank Alan Clemo for finding an anagram for 'Felixstowe workers, unite and fight'. The question posed in the fifth couplet of *Sleepers* was meant to be rhetorical. However, Alan came up with 'When tariffs go, tutored exiles wink', an observation that seems to make economic sense!

THE HIGH WINDOW

The following collections are also available from our website, where further information will be found:
https://thehighwindowpress.com/the-press/

A Slow Blues, Poems 1972-2012 by David Cooke
Angles & Visions by Anthony Costello
The Emigrant's Farewell by James W. Wood
Four American Poets edited by Anthony Costello
Dust by Bethany W. Pope
From Inside by Anthony Howell
The Edge of Seeing by John Duffy
End Phrase by Mario Susko
Bloody, proud and murderous men, adulterers and enemies of God by Steve Ely
Bare Bones by Norton Hodges
Wounded Light by James Russell
Bone Antler Stone by Tim Miller
Wardrobe Blues for a Japanese Lady by Alan Price;
Trodden Before by Patricia McCarthy
Janky Tuk Tuks by Wendy Holborow
Cradle of Bones by Frances Sackett
Of Course, the Yellow Cab by Ken Champion
Forms of Exile: Selected Poems of Marina Tsvetaeva trans. by Belinda Cooke
West South North North South East by Daniel Bennett
Surfaces by Michael Lesher
Man Walking on Water with Tie Askew by Margaret Wilmott
Songs of Realisation by Anthony Howell
Building a Kingdom, New and Selected Poems 1989-2019 by James W. Wood
The Unmaking by Tim O'Leary
Out of the Blue, Selected Poems by Wendy Klein

Man at the Ice House by Alison Mace
Daylight of Seagulls by Alice Allen
Empire of Eden by Tom Laichas